THEN AND THERE SE
CREATED BY MARJOR
GENERAL EDITOR: JO

Elizabeth and Her Court
Third Edition

MARJORIE REEVES

Illustrated from contemporary sources

LONGMAN GROUP UK LIMITED,
Longman House, Burnt Mill, Harlow,
Essex CM20 2JE, England
and Associated Companies throughout the world.

Published in the United States of America by
Longman Inc., New York.

© Longman Group Limited 1956, 1984, Longman Group UK Limited 1990
All rights reserved; no part of this publication
may be reproduced, stored in a retrieval system,
or transmitted in any form or by any means, electronic,
mechanical, photocopying, recording, or otherwise,
without either the prior written permission of the
Publishers or a licence permitting restricted copying
issued by the Copyright Licensing Agency Ltd, 33–34
Alfred Place, London WC1E 7DP.

First published 1956
Second Edition 1984
Third Edition 1990

Set in 11/13 point Rockwell Light (Linotron)
Produced by Longman Group (F.E.), Limited
Printed in Hong Kong

ISBN 0 582 03402 7

Acknowledgements

We are grateful to the following for permission to reproduce photographs: British Library, pages 6, 11, 22, 32, 33; Crown copyright. Reproduced with permission of the Controller of Her Majesty's Stationery Office, page 31; Fotomas Index, pages 47, 60; by gracious permission of Her Majesty the Queen, page 7; Hulton-Deutsch Collection, page 53; The Huntingdon Library, San Marino, California, page 17; Mansell Collection, page 56; by courtesy of The Marquess of Salisbury (photo: Courtauld Institute of Art), page 12; National Portrait Gallery, London, pages 13, 35, 38, 51; Staatliche Kunstsammlungen Kassel, page 23; Victoria & Albert Museum, page 37; by permission of Viscount De L'Isle, VC, KG, from his collection at Penshurst Place, Kent, page 24; Private Collection, page 27.

Cover: Queen Elizabeth I playing the lute by Nicholas Hilliard.
Reproduced by permission of the Trustees of the will of the 8th Earl of Berkeley, Berkeley Castle, Glos.

Contents

	To the reader	4
1	The Princess	5
2	The Queen	10
3	The Court	19
4	The Queen's palaces	29
5	Statesmen and courtiers	34
6	The Queen's progresses	41
7	Foreign visitors	46
8	Court festivities	50
9	Elizabeth and her Parliament	55
10	Epilogue	58
	How do we know?	61
	Glossary	62
	Index	64

To the reader

There are not many kings and queens left in the world now. But in Britain we still have a Queen. She works hard for us, and on special occasions she puts on splendid shows for us. This book is about her great ancestor, Queen Elizabeth I, who lived about 400 years ago. She, too, worked hard for her people, but she particularly liked fine clothes, processions and feasts. Her subjects, both Londoners and country people, loved to see her and her Court parading in all their splendour. She was a wonderful leader and people expected her to look magnificent. People at the time wrote about Elizabeth and her Court and painted pictures. These are called contemporary sources. Those I have used are listed on page 61.

We now use a decimal coinage. In Elizabethan times they used pennies (d) and shillings (s), so that twelve pennies made one shilling and twenty shillings made £1. Wages were rising in this period, but not by very much. An ordinary labourer would get 7d (seven pennies) a day in the summer and only 6d in the winter. Think out why he got less in the winter.

This wage had to cope with rising prices. It has been calculated for us in a special way: two scholars (E. H. Phelps Brown and Sheila V. Hopkins) established a shopping basket of ordinary goods such as one might buy today for a family. They costed it for the latter part of the fifteenth century, and set that at the beginning of their scale as 100. Then they kept on costing it, over and over for the next century. By the beginning of Elizabeth's reign its cost was 230. By 1570 it was 300 and by 1600 it was 459. These last years of the century were the worst for price rises.

Of course not everybody was poor – Lord Burghley's lands brought him an income of £4,000 a year. But he too felt the sting of price rises because rich courtiers were expected to spend in a big way.

Words printed in **heavy black** are explained in the Glossary on page 62.

1 The Princess

When Queen Elizabeth I was a small child her governess wrote to her father saying that the child had neither gown nor **kirtle** nor petticoat and she did not know what would become of her. Her mother, Queen Anne, had been executed when she was only two and her father, King Henry VIII, seemed to dislike her as well and to want to forget about her. Luckily, he changed his mind and sent for her to be brought to Court. There she was much happier. Her step-mother, Queen Catherine, was kind to her and she now had plenty of new clothes.

Doing lessons

Henry VIII had three children: Mary (b. 1516) by his first wife; Elizabeth (b. 1533) by his second wife; and Edward (b. 1537) by his third. When they were still young, Elizabeth and Edward began to do lessons which they enjoyed. Edward began to learn Latin when he was six. By the time Elizabeth was ten she already knew some Latin and had started learning Italian and French. She even wrote letters to Edward in Latin just for fun. On page 6 is a part of one letter in her own handwriting. When she was eleven Elizabeth translated a poem from French into English, wrote it in a book for which she embroidered a cover, and gave it to Queen Catherine for a New Year gift.

Roger Ascham, her tutor, thought his princess was a marvellous pupil. This is what he wrote about her:

> 'She has just passed her sixteenth birthday and shows such dignity and gentlenesss as are wonderfull at her age. She talks French and Italian as well as she does English and has often talked to me readily and well in

Latin, moderately in Greek. When she writes, nothing is more beautiful than her handwriting. She delights as much in music as she is skilful in it.'

Una quidem de re hoc loco satis Illud tantum precor Vt Deus conseruet tuam Maiestatē qua dintiss' incolumem ad nominis sui gloriā regniq vtilitatē. Hatfildiæ 2 februarij

Maiestatis tuæ humilima soror & serua Elizabeth

The end of a letter written by Princess Elizabeth, with her signature. Find the day and month in which it was written and the word 'soror' (sister) which is spelt with an elongated s. To whom did Elizabeth write this letter?

At the Court of King Edward VI

When they were young children the prince and princess must have found life at Court quite splendid, with large numbers of grown-ups who were very polite and kind to them. But as they themselves began to grow up they must have realised that men came to Court to win power, wealth and influence, not to play with royal children. Each courtier wanted power for himself, but some of them found it more convenient to work in packs, called factions, following one or two great men and supporting them in the hopes of lining their own pockets.

The faction leaders wanted to be close to the source of power, to the king and his heirs. They wanted to influence them and use them. Elizabeth soon learned not to give her trust too easily, not to believe people's words and faces. She would have to keep her own counsel if she was to live through, and win.

She learned much in the short reign of her brother Edward. At his death in 1553 some courtiers tried to put

Princess Elizabeth. This portrait was probably painted for Henry VIII in about 1546 when she was thirteen or fourteen. Why do you think the artist put a book in her hand and another large book beside her?

Elizabeth's cousin Lady Jane Grey on the throne. Jane did not want this but men told her this was the only way to continue the Protestant cause in England, by keeping out the Roman Catholic Mary, who should properly have succeeded Edward. Mary's friends soon triumphed, however, and poor Jane was beheaded. Now men began to whisper that Elizabeth herself should take the throne, and Mary began to suspect her of wanting to do this.

Elizabeth in prison

There came a black day in February 1554 when Queen Mary ordered Princess Elizabeth to be imprisoned in the Tower of London. When they brought her by boat to the Traitor's Gate she feared to go up the gloomy steps, saying to the soldiers guarding her: 'I never thought to have come here as a prisoner!'

But Elizabeth kept a cool head and her accusers could prove nothing against her. The people of London began to cry out against keeping the Lady Elizabeth in prison. Queen Mary sent her away into the country, but still as a prisoner. As she travelled in a **litter**, guarded by soldiers, country people came to greet her. At Wycombe the women gave her so many cakes that her litter was full of them. At Rycote they gave her a feast. At last she came to the palace of Woodstock, near Oxford, which was to be her prison.

They did not keep her in a dark cell and feed her on bread and water. After all, she was still the Queen's sister, and heir to the throne. She lived in a rich room with a carved ceiling, painted blue and gold, and she had plenty of servants. But she could not ride out when she wanted to into the green woods and every night 300 soldiers watched from a hill to see that no one got in or out of the palace. Some of her friends came to live at the Bear Inn at Woodstock and she played a dangerous and exciting game with them, sending secret messages backwards and forwards. To pass the time she went on with her studies.

Once, when Elizabeth heard a milkmaid singing cheerfully in the garden, she sighed and said she wished she were a milkmaid whose life was merrier. She wrote letters to the Queen begging to be set free. At last Queen Mary decided she could not keep her at Woodstock any longer and ordered her to come to Court again in April 1555.

Elizabeth free again

Now Princess Elizabeth began to go up in the world. The Queen was still jealous of her but she allowed Elizabeth to live at Hatfield House, not far from London, and to have her own servants. There were good times now. One day she rode out to hunt with twelve huntsmen in green and fifty archers in scarlet boots and yellow caps. Another time she was rowed on the Thames in a boat garlanded with flowers and roofed with green cloth embroidered with golden honeysuckle. Behind her came six boats with her attendants dressed in blue satin and silver. As the bright procession swept by people shouted and waved from the banks, for Elizabeth was more popular than ever now. Soon, many people thought, we shall have our young princess for queen. Messengers often galloped out to Hatfield from London to tell Elizabeth the news of the Court. At last, on the 17th of November 1558, they arrived with the solemn news that Queen Mary was dead. The princess was now Queen Elizabeth I.

Things to do

1. Make two lists, one of the subjects that Elizabeth learnt which you do not do at school, and one of subjects you learn which she did not do. What is different about the education she received from your own?

2. Do you think the events of Elizabeth's childhood might have influenced her when she grew up? In what ways, would you guess?

2 The Queen

Elizabeth I's coronation

Elizabeth was twenty-five years old when she became Queen in 1558. Her coronation was in winter, in the following January. It was snowing a little, but this only made the sparkling jewels and golden collars shine more brightly. There was a great procession from the Tower of London to Westminster. The Queen, dressed in a robe of cloth of gold, was carried in a litter hung with gold brocade. On either side walked gentlemen in crimson velvet and silver. Behind, the Court rode on horseback, dressed in all the colours of the rainbow. The streets were hung with velvet and silk and crowded with people – stout City merchants in furs and ragged vagabonds, rich gentlemen and lean apprentices – all come to rejoice in their new Queen. She had smiles for everyone and her eyes looked everywhere; sometimes she stopped her litter to take some flowers from a poor woman.

It took a long time to reach Westminster for she had to stop often to listen to speeches and watch **pageants**. But she never seemed bored or tired. In Cheapside the Londoners gave Elizabeth 1,000 golden marks (£666) in a crimson satin purse. 'I thank you, my Lord Mayor, and you all,' said Elizabeth. 'Be ye assured that I will be as good unto you as ever Queen was to her people. God thank you all.' Then there was a marvellous shout and a merry noise of trumpets.

Next day Elizabeth was crowned in Westminster Abbey. She carried the **sceptre** and **orb** and smiled a thousand greetings to all her people. The picture on the front cover of this book shows what the Queen looked like. At the feast in Westminster Hall a knight, called the Queen's Cham-

Part of Elizabeth's coronation procession, drawn by someone who saw it.

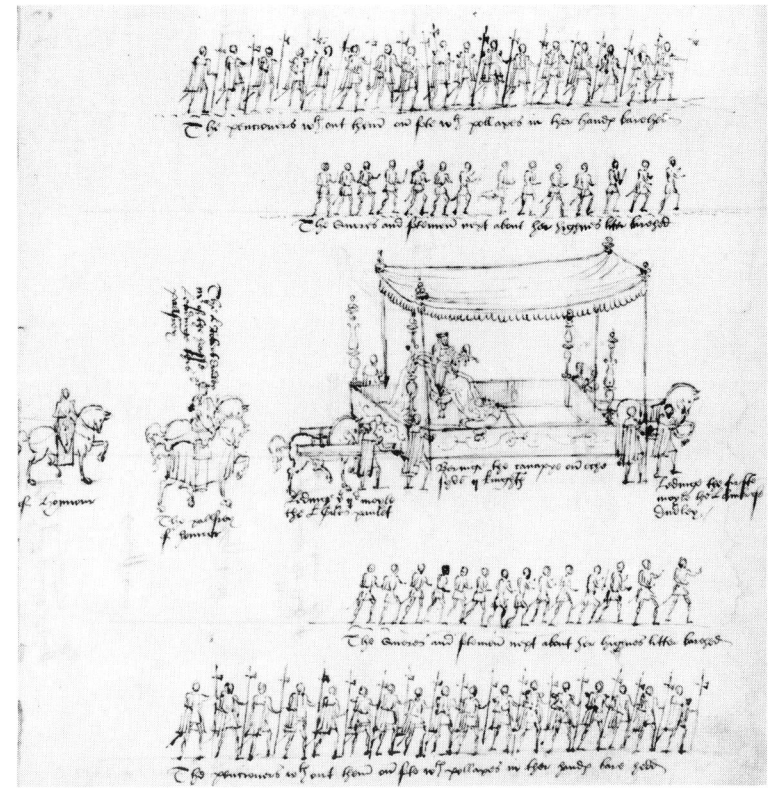

pion, rode into the hall in full armour on a horse covered with cloth of gold. In a loud voice he challenged the Queen's enemies to come and fight him. Of course no one answered; we shall hear about real enemies later.

What Elizabeth looked like

What did Elizabeth really look like? Writers who saw her tried to describe her and artists painted her in colour. Elizabeth herself thought some of the portraits ugly and commanded that no one was to paint her without her permission. Her later portraits show her as she wanted her people to see her: magnificent, glorious, powerful. Artists had to paint her covered with jewels, quite young-looking

11

Queen Elizabeth in 1585, painted probably by William Segar. How old was she in 1585?

and accompanied by signs of her greatness. In one picture she wears a **pelican** ornament because, as the pelican is supposed to peck its own breast and let the blood run to feed her young, so Elizabeth looked after her people. In the picture above she has a stuffed **ermine** on her sleeve because the ermine was a sign of royalty. Look at the elaborate ruff, part of the fashion of the day. In the picture on page 13 she also has a huge ruff and a **farthingale**. Why has Elizabeth been painted with her feet on a map of England?

This portrait of Elizabeth, painted by a Dutch painter, Gheeraerts, about 1592, probably marks her visit to Sir Henry Lee at Ditchley (Oxfordshire). Later portraits show Queen Elizabeth as much younger looking. Why was this, do you think?

So it is difficult to know when writers and painters were being honest and when they were just flattering the Queen. Compare what one writer said about her with her portraits on pages 12 and 13:

'She was a lady of great beauty, of decent **stature** and of an excellent shape. Her skin was of pure white and her hair of a yellow colour; her eyes were beautiful and lively. Her face was adorned with wonderful and sweet beauty and majesty. This beauty lasted till her middle age, though it declined.'

Dressing must have been a long affair. First there was a white smock to put on and then a tight bodice stiffened with whalebone and a great petticoat stiffened with hoops of whalebone or steel which was called a farthingale. Over this foundation came all the rich clothes – first an elaborate petticoat, then a kirtle, which was a dress in two parts (a bodice and a skirt, often open all down the front). Finally the Queen might put on a top gown, also open down the front. It was difficult to keep the great collars stiff, but Elizabeth sent for a woman from Holland, Mistress Dinghen Vanderplasse, who knew the secret of making proper starch. She would teach this secret for £5. Even so, when fashionable ladies got caught in the rain, their fine ruffs would flop round their necks like wet rags.

Elizabeth was proud of her reddish-fair hair. She wore it frizzed and decorated with little jewelled ships and other ornaments in it. When her hair faded she wore auburn-red wigs. Notice how she is covered with embroidery and jewels. On her dresses you might find peacocks and butterflies, the ermine and the **phoenix**, roses and other flowers, suns and moons – everything you could think of embroidered in brilliant colours or sparkling in necklaces.

Her clothes were sweet-scented and she liked to carry posies of flowers. Elizabeth hated bad smells – and there were plenty in those days. 'Tush, man,' she said to a courtier one day, 'your boots stink.' She was delighted when her godson invented a real flush lavatory for her.

New Year presents

Courtiers who wished to please the Queen gave her New Year presents of things to wear. Elizabeth carefully recorded all these gifts. These are a few of the many presents she received:

> the first pair of black silk stockings in England (1560),
> a white satin bodice embroidered with gold flowers,
> a petticoat of yellow satin patterned in silver and **tawny** silk with a silver fringe,
> a white satin petticoat lined with carnation, laid over with silver lace, fringed with silver and carnation,
> a silver kirtle embroidered with gold and silver flowers,
> a bodice of peach-coloured satin, laid with Venice gold lace and lined with orange,
> a tawny satin nightgown edged with Venice lace, furred with black fur,
> a pair of perfumed gloves with 24 diamond and gold buttons,
> a fan of white feathers with a golden handle, one side decorated with two emeralds, and the other with diamonds and rubies.

Many people gave her jewels. Here are a few of those she received:

> a squirrel in gold, with 3 sparks of diamonds, 3 of emeralds and 4 of rubies,
> a mother of pearl swan decorated with small diamonds,
> a necklace of golden roses with a diamond in each and a pearl hanging from it,
> a golden lily, set with diamonds, with 3 pearls hanging from it.

Sometimes her servants gave her quaint things like:

> a figure of St George made in marzipan,
> a white bear of gold and mother of pearl holding a ragged staff wherein is a clock,

6 small gold toothpicks,
18 larks in a cage.

Elizabeth was a great one for eating sweets, so she often got a jewelled **comfit** box as a present. She ruined her teeth because of eating sweets.

Elizabeth's inventory

With all this present-giving, you will not be surprised to hear that when she died in 1603, aged 70, Elizabeth left 3,000 dresses. A short while before, in 1600, she had an **inventory** made of her clothes. Here are some of the things in the list:

Robes	99	Petticoats	125
French Gowns	102	Cloaks	96
Round Gowns	67	Bodices	85
Loose Gowns	100	Kirtles	126
Fans	27		

One of these fans, made of red and white feathers with a golden handle, was a present from Sir Francis Drake. Many of the gowns were very expensive, for silks and velvets had to be brought from Italy or France. Even plain satin cost 14 shillings a yard (remember that quite well off people in those days earned a shilling a day). Rich stuffs with gold and silver thread woven into them were extravagantly dear.

How Elizabeth spent her day

But Elizabeth was a great deal more than just a gorgeous peacock. One writer tells us how she spent her day. First she had some time at her prayers, then she did government business, reading letters and dictating answers or talking to her ministers. Then she would walk in the garden or watch her courtiers playing tennis or go out into the country to hunt or hawk. These hunting expeditions often ended

in a court picnic under the greenwood tree. Here is a picture of one in 1573. It is a woodcut from Turberville's *The Booke of Hunting.*

Every day Elizabeth did some study. She was glad that she had studied so well as a girl, for when people made speeches to her in Latin (which was the international language of that time) she understood and could even reply in Latin. When foreign princes or **ambassadors** came she could even talk to them in French or Italian. She went on studying all her life and could talk learnedly to bishops. Yet she loved music and dancing and in the evenings would amuse herself with these or with a game of chess.

Elizabeth kept power in her own hands. She decided which of her courtiers she would favour and which of her **statesmen** she would listen to when deciding the best ways to keep peace. She could be gorgeous herself and yet careful (even stingy) about money, frivolous and yet serious-minded, almost young and old at the same time.

Things to do

1. Elizabeth's coronation procession went through Cheapside, Strand, Whitehall to Westminster. When the Queen today goes in procession to Westminster Abbey, what route does she take? Find a map of London and trace out the two routes.

2. What are the sceptre and orb?

3. Describe an Elizabethan farthingale, kirtle and ruff. You could add drawings.

4. Look carefully at the hunting picture on page 17. How many different things are happening? Describe them.

5. Why do you think courtiers gave Elizabeth presents? Why did she keep lists?

3 The Court

A German visitor comes to the Court

Curious foreigners are very useful people, for they often write down what they see and they notice things we might miss. In 1598 a German visitor named Hentzner was much excited because he actually got into the Queen's presence. This is how he described the great occasion:

> 'We were admitted into the Presence **Chamber**, hung with rich tapestry and the floor, after the English fashion, strewed with hay; at the door stood a gentleman in velvet, with a gold chain, whose office was to introduce to the Queen any person of distinction that came to wait upon her. In the same hall were a great number of counsellors of state and gentlemen who waited the Queen's coming out to go to prayers. First came barons, earls, knights of the Garter, all richly dressed and bare-headed; next came the Chancellor, bearing the Seals in a red silk purse, between two others, one carrying the royal sceptre, the other the sword of state in a red **scabbard**; next came the Queen, in the 65th year of her age, very majestic, her face fair but wrinkled, her eyes small yet black and pleasant, her nose a little hooked, her teeth black (from the English habit of too great use of sugar). She had in her ears two pearls with very rich drops; she wore false hair and that red; upon her head she had a small crown and she had on a necklace of exceeding fine jewels. Her air was stately, her manner of speaking mild and obliging. That day she was dressed in white silk, bordered with pearls of the size of beans, and over it a **mantle** of black silk shot

with silver threads, with a long train. As she went along she spoke very graciously to one and another in English, French and Italian. Wherever she turned her face as she was going along, everybody fell down on their knees. The ladies of the Court followed, very handsome and well-shaped, for the most part dressed in white. She was guarded on each side by 50 gentlemen with gilt battle-axes.'

Preparing the Queen's dinner

While the Queen was in the chapel Hentzner watched preparations for dinner:

'We saw her table set with the following solemnity: a gentleman entered the room bearing a rod and with him one with a tablecloth which, after they had both kneeled three times with the utmost veneration, he spread upon the table. Then came two others with a salt-cellar, a plate and bread which they placed on the table with the same ceremonies. (At last came a countess dressed in white silk who, after she had bowed three times in the most graceful manner, rubbed the plates with bread and salt.) Then the Yeoman of the Guard entered, bare-headed, clothed in scarlet with a golden rose upon their backs, bringing in 24 dishes, served on gilt plates. These were placed on the table while a lady-taster gave each of the guards a mouthful to eat of the dish he had brought, for fear of any poison. During the time that this guard, which has the tallest and stoutest men that can be found in all England, were bringing dinner, twelve trumpets and two kettle-drums made the hall ring for half an hour. At the end of this ceremonial, the Queen's ladies appeared and with great solemnity lifted the food off the table and carried it into the Queen's private chamber, for the Queen dines and sups with very few attendants.'

Perhaps the Queen and her ladies liked to eat in private because they had such good appetites. We know they had beef, bread and beer for breakfast because Elizabeth made her servants keep careful accounts of all the food eaten. Here is the list for just one dinner:

round of brawn	sirloin of beef	4 joints of veal
2 geese	6 hens	6 rabbits
6 woodcocks	4 partridges	1 pheasant
1½ doz. pigeons	4 snipe	3 doz. larks

Butter, eggs, spices, fruit, bread, ale, white and red wine, rose-water.

The Queen's servants

The Court was managed by three great officers: the Master of the Horse, the Lord High Steward and the Lord Great Chamberlain. Under them were many officers and servants. There were gentlemen **ushers** and **grooms** of the **Privy** Chamber and Outer Chamber, ladies of the Privy Chamber, carvers, cupbearers, pages and Yeomen of the Guard. There were clerks of the counting-house and jewel-house, a Master of the Revels, Children of the Chapel, musicians and huntsmen. There were cooks of the kitchen and servants of the bake-house, pantry, cellar, buttery, spicery, **chandlery**, confectionery, larder, poultry, scalding-house, pastry and scullery.

So there was an army of people, great and small, in the Court, each one with his or her own place or title. We know about them because Elizabeth hated to waste money and so she made her servants keep careful account of all they spent. We still have some of these account-books showing that she checked and signed them herself (see page 22). This is a piece of one account made by the Keeper of the Queen's Purse.

Paid for:
Jewels	£2294–3–3½
Horses	£524–3–4

Elizabeth's signature in one of her account books.

Lute-strings	£74–3–4
Perfumes	£68–7–1
Binding of 4 books	£1–6–8
Curtains for Privy Chambers	£6-8-0
One **sackbut** for Queen's use	£15–9–0
Food for the Queen's Deer	£145–3–8
Payments made to the Queen's silkwoman	£702–11–0¼
Payments made to David Smith, embroiderer	£203–15–7
Payments made to Peter Trinder, goldsmith	£32–15–0
Payments made to Mrs Tayler, Queen's laundress	£4–0–0

Music and dancing at Court

Elizabeth generally gave audience to specially honoured people in her Privy Chamber. Here her close advisers, the Privy Councillors, and her Maids of Honour would stand round her. The Maids were girls from noble families. They had to play, sing or read to the Queen and dance whenever she commanded it. In the Privy Chamber there were always musicians ready to play. The Maids had a hard life, for they had to do whatever the Queen commanded and even marry the young men that she chose for them.

In the first days of Elizabeth's reign slow and stately dances, such as one called the pavane, were popular. Then new ones, very quick and lively, came into fashion

Elizabeth receiving foreign ambassadors in her Privy Chamber, painted by an unknown German artist about 1565.

from France, especially the galliard and the volta (see the picture on page 24) in which the dancers leapt into the air and whirled round very fast.

Here is a foreign visitor's account of the dancing:

'The men **donned** their hats, although otherwise no one may put on his hat in the Queen's Chamber. The dancers danced behind one another and all wore gloves. While dancing they often curtsied to one another and every time the men bowed before their partners they **doffed** their hats. Slender and beautiful were the women and magnificently robed. Meanwhile the Queen chatted and jested most amiably with young and old. Pointing her finger at one gentleman she told him there was a smut on his face. She offered to wipe it off with her handkerchief but he removed it himself.'

23

Dancing the volta at Court, painted at the time by an unknown artist. The two people in the centre may be Elizabeth and the Earl of Leicester. What instruments are the musicians playing? Do all the men wear their hats?

Although Queen Elizabeth could be merry like this in her Privy Chamber, everyone at Court had to behave according to a solemn **etiquette**. When she was angry everyone trembled. Yet she was often gracious and deliberately charming, for she very much wanted the love and loyalty of her people, and knew that she would have to work for it.

The Queen and Londoners

The Londoners adored her because she appeared among

them so often. Here is a description of a river festival on St George's Day:

> 'After supper the Queen was rowed up and down the Thames, hundreds of boats rowing round her and thousands of people thronging at the water-side to look on her Majesty, rejoicing to see her and enjoying the music. For the trumpets blew, drums beat, flutes played, guns were fired and **squibs** hurled up in the air. Thus showing herself so freely to her people, the Queen made herself dear and acceptable to them.'

One July, when the Queen was at Greenwich Palace, the City Companies of London marched down to Greenwich in coats of velvet and chains of gold and armed with **muskets, pikes** and **halberds**. In the park they **skirmished** for her entertainment. The Queen thanked them heartily, whereupon immediately she was given the greatest shout as ever was heard, with hurling up of caps, and the Queen was very merry. Later a summer-house was made for the Queen in the park in which to feast and watch a tournament between six great lords. Here through the long summer evening she **banqueted** and watched plays and fireworks. How beautiful it must have looked in the blue dusk, with all the Court, like gorgeous, jewelled moths, gleaming in the yellow candle-light!

Tournaments

The day of Elizabeth's accession, 17th November, was a holiday in all the London schools and at Westminster there was a **joust** in which noblemen entertained the Queen in mock fights. They fought on horse-back with **lances**, then with swords and then on foot with pikes. The fighting was not serious and it was really an occasion for dressing up. Here is a description of jousters in 1581:

> 'First the Earl of Arundel entered the **Tilt Yard**, in gilt armour, with 4 pages and 22 gentlemen all dressed in

cloaks and **hose** of crimson velvet, laid with gold lace, **doublets** of yellow satin, hats of crimson velvet with yellow feathers and yellow silk stockings. He had 6 trumpeters and 31 yeomen all in crimson and yellow.

After him rode the Lord Windsor, with 4 pages and 24 gentlemen in short cloaks of scarlet, lined with orange taffeta and laid with silver lace, with doublets and hose of orange satin and black velvet caps with silver bands and white feathers. He had 4 trumpeters, 4 grooms and 36 yeomen, all in orange, silver and black.

Then rode Master Philip Sidney, in armour partly blue and the rest gilt. His 4 pages were dressed in silver and gold and his gentlemen in yellow velvet and silver ...'

So the gorgeous procession went on.

Maundy Thursday

In the Bible, when Christ wanted to show he was a lord and master who could be humble and serve his followers, he washed his disciples' feet. You can read the story in the thirteenth chapter of the Gospel of John. Christ told his followers that they were to follow his example, so here in England the most powerful person in the land, Queen Elizabeth, did just that. On Maundy Thursday (the Thursday before Easter) she washed the feet of as many poor people as the years of her age. We have a description of this ceremony in 1572:

'Her Majesty came into the hall, and after some singing and prayers made and the Gospel of Christ's washing His disciples' feet read, she, kneeling down upon the cushions under the feet of the poor women, first washed one foot of everyone in several basins of warm water and sweet flowers, then wiped, crossed and kissed it. When her Majesty had thus gone through

Queen Elizabeth going to a wedding in London in 1600, probably painted by Robert Peake. The artist has made her look quite young. How old was she in 1600?

the whole number of 39, she went back to the first again and gave each a pair of shoes, then a plate with fish and bread to eat and finally a white purse with 39 pence and a red purse with 20 shillings.'

The Queen still gives purses of money to selected people on Maundy Thursday in our own times.

St George's Day

On St George's Day the Queen went in procession to her chapel with all the Knights of the Garter dressed in their rich garter robes. Afterwards there was a great feast at

27

which the Queen sometimes made new Knights of the Garter. This ceremony still goes on in our own days, as well.

If you think that all these ceremonies and festivals were just to amuse the Queen, you would be wrong. Elizabeth wanted to make a great figure of herself. She meant to impress foreign ambassadors and give people at home a Queen they could be enthusiastic about and therefore loyal to. The splendid Court was all part of her purpose to be a larger-than-life Queen.

Things to do

1. Read Hentzner's descriptions again on pages 19 and 20 and then answer these questions:
   a) What was odd about the floor of the Presence Chamber?
   b) What were the seals which the chancellor carried?
   c) Look up the word **flattery** in your dictionary and then say whether you think Hentzner's description of Elizabeth was an honest one or only flattery.
   d) Why do you think there was all that fuss about laying the Queen's dinner-table?

2. Look at the list of court servants on page 21. Write down what you think each had to do.

3. What does the piece from the Queen's accounts on pages 21–22 tell us about the things she liked and what she liked to do?

4. Read again what happened on Maunday Thursday on pages 26–27. Why were there 39 women? How many men or women would there be when the Queen does the same thing today?

4 The Queen's palaces

Whitehall Palace

Nearly all the palaces in which Elizabeth I held her Court have since been pulled down and Buckingham Palace had not yet been built. So, in imagining Elizabeth's Court we have to use old pictures and descriptions written at the time. Her chief palace was in Westminster. It stood in Whitehall by the Thames. You must imagine all the buildings of today cleared away and the palace there instead, with its archways and courtyards, its turrets and multitude of chimneys, its tilt yard, garden and orchard. A stately stairway led down to the river and on the water the royal barge always waited, ready to take the Queen wherever she pleased. It was rowed by her own special water-men, dressed in scarlet.

In the Queen's palaces the Great Hall was the most important part. As you read this book picture to yourself the grand ceremonies taking place in a hall like the one at Hampton Court (see page 31). Then there were several Presence Chambers in which the Queen received visitors. The Privy Chamber was her own sitting-room. Close by were her bedchamber and rooms for her ladies. In some palaces there was a long gallery in which courtiers and visitors strolled and talked while waiting for the Queen. There was always a chapel in the palace and a great many rooms for courtiers and servants as well as vast kitchens.

What Hentzner saw

When Hentzner went to Whitehall Palace he said the following things were worth looking at:

1. The Royal Library, well stored with Greek, Latin,

French and Italian books, bound in velvet of different colours, though chiefly red, with clasps of gold and silver and some with pearls and precious stones in their covers.
2. Two little silver cabinets of exquisite work in which the Queen keeps her papers.
3. The Queen's bed, made of woods of different colours, with quilts of silk, velvet, gold, silver and embroidery.
4. A little chest, ornamented with pearls, in which the Queen keeps her jewellery.

The Queen's bed was splendid. It was enclosed in curtains of silver cloth trimmed with gold and silver lace and embroidered with 347 sprigs of flowers. The ceiling was of white satin, with six bunches of ostrich feathers spangled with gold above it. This gorgeous bed took to pieces and travelled round with the Queen.

Richmond and Hampton Court Palaces

Elizabeth probably enjoyed getting away from the smells of London. It was pleasant to set forth on the Thames where many a swan came floating, white as snow, and sail up the river to her palace of Richmond. This has now disappeared but there is an old picture of it on page 32.

Further up the river still was Elizabeth's palace of Hampton Court. This had been built by the great archbishop and cardinal, Thomas Wolsey. Then Elizabeth's father, Henry VIII, took it over and made it into one of the finest palaces in England. You can still visit it today. Kings and queens since Elizabeth have altered it but the Great Hall is still very much as King Henry built it and Elizabeth used it.

Underneath are the beer and wine cellars and the great kitchen (11 metres long and 8 metres wide) which would have been full of cooks running here and there, and of great joints roasting when the Queen and Court arrived.

The Great Hall at Hampton Court.

Richmond Palace as it looked at the end of the sixteenth century.

There would be about 500 people to feed and while they were feasting in the Great Hall there would be a procession of serving-men all the way up the stairs from the kitchen with hot, steaming dishes.

The Queen's other palaces

Sometimes Elizabeth went out to Windsor Castle which looked then as magnificent on its hill as it does now. She often went down the river to her palace of Greenwich or Placentia where, you remember, she feasted in the summer banqueting house in the park.

Finally, away in Surrey, Elizabeth had an elegant summer palace called Nonesuch (None like it). People thought it was a fairy palace with its turrets, shining windows and bright copper **cupolas**. Here and at Hampton Court there were elaborate gardens. The paths were covered with sand and there were fountains, statues and yew trees cut into shapes of birds and beasts. The flower beds were edged with tiny hedges and laid out in patterns. On hot summer days they blazed with carnations and poppies,

The Queen arriving in her coach at Nonesuch Palace, from an engraving made in 1582.

lilies, marigolds and roses. Elizabeth and her ladies walked along shady paths arched over with lime trees or sat in arbours of sweetbriar and honeysuckle, while the fountains tinkled coolly and the air was scented with lavender and rosemary.

When London began to get hot and smelly in the early summer Elizabeth was glad to roll away in her coach to Nonesuch.

Things to do

1. Draw a picture of the Queen's bed using the description on page 30, or of the Queen's garden at Nonesuch (pages 32–33).

2. Using the picture above, describe the Queen's arrival at Nonesuch. Can you work out what the Latin words mean?

3. Why did Elizabeth need so many palaces?

5 Statesmen and courtiers

Elizabeth's chief statesmen

Though Elizabeth was young when she became Queen, she chose serious and wise men to be her advisers. She knew that there were enemies at home and abroad and that she would need very good advice to avoid walking into the traps they set for her. One of the first men she called to her Council was Sir William Cecil. He had helped her when she had been in danger as a girl and now he became her faithful watchdog. When she made him a Councillor she wrote to him:

> 'This judgement I have of you that you will not be **corrupted** with any gift and that you will be faithful to the State, and that, without respect of my private will, you will give me that counsel that you think best.'

Cecil knew that the kings of Spain and France were watching eagerly to see how they could get Elizabeth into their power. Philip of Spain had been married to Queen Mary and perhaps would have liked to marry Elizabeth now, while the French king wanted to give her a French husband. They both wanted England to turn Roman Catholic again. If they could not make her do what they wanted, they planned to depose her and make her cousin, Mary, Queen of Scots, queen instead. Cecil kept Elizabeth out of these dangers, for she did not fall into the power of either Spain or France, see-sawing first towards one, and at the last minute changing back again. In England itself Cecil seemed to have eyes and ears everywhere to discover plotters and stop their schemes. Elizabeth rewarded him by making him Lord Burghley and always asking his advice first.

William Cecil, after he became Lord Burghley, probably painted by the Dutch artist, Gheeraerts, in 1585.

Another of Elizabeth's faithful statesmen was Sir Francis Walsingham. He was a dark-faced, serious man who did not like to be frivolous and would not join in the merry-making at Court.

But although she listened to Cecil and Walsingham, Elizabeth herself decided what to do and did it her own way. She preferred to put off a final decision as long as possible and keep people guessing. Often, if she did nothing, the problem would go away. She was keen on saving money whenever she could. Altogether she was very successful in keeping England out of wars and keeping people loyal at home.

The one occasion when war really threatened was during the great Armada of 1588. England had sent troops abroad to fight in France and the Netherlands, and English pirates attacked Spanish and Portuguese treasure fleets on the seas, but now here was the possibility of invasion. English guns, English ships, English seamen and English weather (perhaps the most important) combined to defeat the Armada, but it had been a fright. You can read more about this in another *Then and There* book.

Young courtiers

Elizabeth's statesmen were not all grave and serious. She was clever enough to see that a man who looked on the surface just a dandy might have some brains as well. One day a young man came to Court who danced most elegantly. The Queen asked his name and found it was Christopher Hatton. He became a favourite courtier, but people were surprised when Elizabeth made him Lord Chancellor, chief of all the judges in the land, when he was only forty-seven. On his first day as Lord Chancellor he rode to court with forty gentlemen in blue satin coats and gold chains, but people found that he had a good head as well as fine clothes, for he was a wise Lord Chancellor. He still liked to dance, however, and the Queen liked to watch him.

Young men came to Court to be Elizabeth's Gentlemen Pensioners. Many came from well-known families but were themselves poor. The way to get on in Elizabeth's time was to find a nobleman who would be your **patron** and push you forward. Sometimes you put all your money into a fine suit of clothes, hoping to catch the Queen's eye. If, with the help of your patron you got the Queen's support she could give you some job (usually one which had little work to do) which put a lot of money in your pocket, and made you important. Courtiers were greedy for favours and so they flattered Elizabeth all they could. She let them do it because this showed her power over them.

Miniature of a Young Man by Nicholas Hilliard. Painting miniatures was popular in Elizabethan times and Hilliard was the greatest miniaturist or limner (from illuminate). He was appointed goldsmith and limner to the Queen and painted many pictures of her and her courtiers. This picture's Latin motto reads *Dat poenas laudata fides* which translates 'My praised faith causes my pain'. What do you think this means?

Courtiers' clothes

It was not only the Queen and her ladies who dressed extravagantly. The men looked like vain peacocks strutting about. They copied the latest fashions from France and Italy and sometimes spent £100 on one get-up. Their doublets, hose and cloaks were of silk, velvet or satin in gorgeous colours, decorated with gold and silver lace. Doublets had large sleeves, puffed and slashed, while hose were short and sometimes enormously padded out. Ruffs round the neck grew bigger and bigger, until the wearers almost sailed away in the wind. Elizabeth tried in vain to limit their size. Silk stockings – very expensive – were all the rage; shoes had rosettes or were embroidered with gold or silver; hats had huge bunches of bright feathers. Embroidered and perfumed gloves came into fashion when Edward de Vere, Earl of Oxford, gave the Queen a pair he had brought from Italy. They pleased her so much that she had her portrait painted wearing them.

Favourite courtiers

Sir Robert Dudley was a great favourite. He was a princely man and Elizabeth thought him most handsome. As soon as she became Queen she made him Master of the Horse.

Robert Dudley, Earl of Leicester, painted sometime between 1575 and 1580.

He looked very fine on horseback, especially when jousting in a tournament. Later she made him Earl of Leicester; he flattered her and made wonderful entertainments for her.

Sir Walter Raleigh was adventurous but poor. When he came to Court of course he wanted to catch the Queen's eye. One day he wrote with a diamond on a window-pane which he knew Elizabeth would see when she passed by:

'Fain would I climb, yet fear to fall'
(meaning: I very much want to climb . . .)

When the Queen saw it, she added another line with her diamond ring:

'If thy heart fail thee, climb not at all.'

Raleigh was not afraid to try to climb into Elizabeth's favour and he succeeded well, for he was a fine-looking man, six feet tall, dark and handsome. He wrote poetry, made elegant speeches and was the kind of bold adventurer the Queen liked.

One of Elizabeth's most loved courtiers was Sir Philip Sidney. He was a poet and a brave soldier. But when he was only thirty-two he was killed in Holland when fighting to help the Dutch get their freedom from Spain. Everyone in England, from the Queen downwards, grieved for his death and many poets wrote in his honour.

The Faerie Queen

Elizabeth's courtiers aimed at excelling in many things: they tilted and fought and adventured over the seas to new lands; they also sang, danced and wrote poetry. Edmund Spenser, a friend of Raleigh's, wrote a long poem called the 'Faerie Queen' which he **dedicated** to Elizabeth in these words:

'To the most high, mighty and magnificent Empress, renowned for piety, virtue and all gracious government, Elizabeth, by the grace of God Queen of England, France and Ireland and of Virginia, her most humble servant Edmund Spenser doth in all humility dedicate, present and consecrate these his labours to live with the eternity of her fame.'

Although the poem tells stories of imaginary knights and

ladies, the Faerie Queen is really meant to be Elizabeth herself. She rewarded Spenser with a pension of £50 a year (remember that you could live well on a shilling a week, which was £2.60 a year). Spenser pictures Elizabeth sitting on a rich throne:

> 'With royal robes and gorgeous array,
> A maiden queen, that shone as **Titan's** ray,
> In glistening gold and **peerless** precious stones.'

Many other writers wrote in praise of Elizabeth and dedicated their books to her. They certainly hoped for a reward, but also they wrote because poetry was in the air and people enjoyed beautiful words.

Things to do

1. Read again what Elizabeth wrote to Cecil (page 34). Put it into your own words.

2. Sir Christopher Hatton once said: 'The Queen did fish for men's souls and had so sweet a bait that no one could escape her net.' What do you think he meant?

3. Draw an Elizabethan courtier in his doublet, hose, cloak and ruff, *or* write an account of the difference between Elizabethan dress (men's and women's) and ours today.

4. There is a famous story about Raleigh (clue: a cloak) and one about Sidney (clue: a cup of water). Find these stories and write them in your own words.

5. On page 39 Elizabeth is called Queen of Virginia. Where is Virginia and why do we connect Raleigh with it?

6. Hilliard said about the painter's job: 'Now know that all painting imitateth nature . . . of all things the perfection is to imitate the face of mankind.' Did artists really try to imitate Elizabeth's face? Why not?

6 The Queen's progresses

Travelling round the country

Every year in summer Elizabeth went on a tour round the country which was called a progress. She did this in order that as many people as possible should see their Queen and so become more loyal to her. Besides the Queen and her Court, a whole host of servants went too and they often took beds and a great deal of furniture. Think of packing all those enormous stiffened dresses and ruffs! The roads were rough and the hundreds of carts often got stuck in the mud. But Elizabeth enjoyed herself, even if the courtiers and servants grumbled.

The Queen rode on horseback or in a litter or a coach. The first coach in England was built for Elizabeth by a Dutchman. Along the road country people flocked to see her. She liked this and often stopped to let them speak or offer nosegays. One writer says:

> 'Men and women, country people and children came joyfully and without fear to see her. Her ears were open to complaints. She would not allow the poorest to be shut away from her. She took with her own hands and read with the greatest goodness the **petitions** of the lowest **rustic**.'

Elizabeth's visits

When a town heard that the Queen was to pay a visit, there was a great scurry round to clean the streets and decorate the houses. When she arrived they rang the bells, produced pageants and recited long poems or speeches to her. When she visited Coventry the citizens gave her

£100 in a silver cup. Elizabeth said: 'It is a good present, £100 in gold! I have few such gifts.' The Mayor replied boldly: 'If it please your Grace, there is a great deal more in it.' 'What is that?' said she. 'It is the hearts of all your loving subjects.' 'We thank you, Mr Mayor,' said the Queen, 'it is a great deal more indeed.'

When she visited Sandwich in 1573 the townsfolk garlanded the streets with flowers and placed a great gilt lion and dragon at the gates. The wives of the chief men gave her a banquet of 160 different dishes. She was merry and ate much, refusing to let her taster try the dishes first against poison. This pleased the wives greatly.

In 1578 at Norwich sixty of the finest young men in the city rode out to meet her in black satin and yellow, followed by the mayor and officials in scarlet and violet gowns. Entertainments were arranged by a man named Thomas Churchyard. One of his inventions was a little coach in which rode a small boy dressed as **Mercury** in blue satin and gold, with wings on his hat and heels. The coach came skimming along right up to the Queen. Then Mercury hopped out, made a deep bow and recited a long poem to Elizabeth.

What the Queen saw

Elizabeth's sharp eyes looked round her as her coach bumped along the rough roads. She noticed a great many tramps on the road. Some looked like real rogues, but many were poor people who had been turned out of their homes by rich landlords who wanted to make pastures for large flocks of sheep. Once a crowd of these tramps swarmed round her coach begging for help. When she returned to London Elizabeth talked to her Council about how to stop rich men from taking too much land and how to find work for poor people. Then new laws were passed in Parliament. These laws were hard on real tramps but did try to find food and work for the poor.

A sixteenth-century woodcut of beggars.

Visiting great noblemen

It was a great honour for a noble lord to entertain the Queen but it was also a huge expense. Mountains of food and rivers of wine had to be provided. Here is a list of some of the food bought by Lord North when the Queen stayed for three days:

> 67 sheep, 34 pigs, 4 stags and 16 bucks used for 176 pasties, 1,200 chickens, 363 capons, 33 geese, 6 turkeys, 237 dozen pigeons, many pheasants and partridges, cartloads of oysters and fish, 2,500 eggs, 430 lbs. of butter.

When Elizabeth visited the Earl of Leicester's castle at Kenilworth the entertainments were so marvellous that several people wrote about them. She was greeted by a huge man dressed as **Hercules** who presented her with the castle keys. Then she came to a stretch of water where the Lady of the Lake welcomed her in verses. There were acrobatics, fireworks and dancing.

When she visited the Earl of Hertford at Elvetham, he

A drawing of the entertainment at Elvetham. Find the three islands, the Queen on her throne and Neptune with Tritons blowing horns, drawing the ship full of girls.

had 300 men at work beforehand enlarging the house and digging a lake shaped like a half-moon, with three islands on it, one like a ship, one like a fort and one like a snail. The Queen sat on a throne by the lake and **Neptune** came through the water drawing a ship full of singing girls who gave Elizabeth two jewels. While the Queen and the Court feasted in the garden there were fireworks from the islands in the lake. When Elizabeth went away the Fairy Queen appeared with her maidens singing a song which ended like this:

'O come again, world's starbright eye,
Whose presence doth adorn the sky,
O come again, sweet beauty's sun,
When thou art gone, our joys are done.'

Things to do

1. Why were the people of Sandwich pleased that Elizabeth ate their banquet straight away?

2. Find out who Mercury, Hercules and Neptune were. Why did people play their parts?

3. Do you think Elizabeth pleased the people who entertained her? Give reasons for your answer. Was it important for the Queen to go on progress?

7 Foreign visitors

The Queen's suitors

The visits of foreign ambassadors and princes gave Queen Elizabeth a splendid chance to show off the magnificence of her Court. Visitors came very early in her reign, partly out of curiosity and partly to solve the great question of the day – whether Elizabeth would marry. Almost as soon as she was Queen the Prince of Sweden arrived to try and marry her and after him came the King of Denmark's nephew. But Elizabeth was rather like the princess in the fairy-tale who refuses all her rich **suitors**. Parliament begged her to marry but she would not.

So long as she kept them guessing, her suitors went on hoping that she would say yes and this meant that they would not take sides against her. So she wanted princes to go on asking her to marry. Eric of Sweden tried for two years to persuade her. He sent her eighteen horses and a whole ship-load of other presents. Later, two French princes, brothers of the King of France, came as suitors, one after the other. Elizabeth knew that it was very important for her to keep friendly with the French king, for she had many enemies abroad. So she did not want to offend the princes. When they arrived she did not say 'No' at once but entertained them royally and gave them no answer at all.

The second of these princes, the Duke of Alencon, slipped over to England in disguise. Elizabeth nicknamed him her 'little frog'. When he went away he told her that he was the most faithful and affectionate slave in the world. Then he sent over his secretary, Marchaumont. Elizabeth took him down the river to Deptford to a banquet on board

Sir Francis Drake's ship the *Golden Hind*. Going on board, the Queen's purple and gold garter slipped off her leg. Marchaumont picked it up. The Queen asked for it back saying that she had nothing else to keep her stocking up but later she sent the garter to Marchaumont who triumphantly gave it to his master as a favour from the Queen.

But in the end she did not marry a French prince. Many English people did not want this marriage because he would be a **Catholic**. They remembered the times when Queen Mary had had a Catholic husband, Philip of Spain, and they preferred the **Protestant** religion of England. Elizabeth cared very much about keeping the loyalty of her people. So she gave up the French marriage and never married at all. She may have felt that a husband would interfere with her power. Thus she was often called the Virgin Queen.

Visitors from Russia

One day there came riding through the streets of London men in strange fur hats and coats. They were ambassadors from Ivan, Tsar of Muscovy (Russia) and they brought rich presents of furs and yellow amber for Elizabeth. Russia was in those days a strange far-off land which English sailors

Foreign visitors. This is how the people of Muscovy dressed.

tried to reach through icy northern seas that froze solid in winter. They wanted to get there partly because there were rich things to buy and partly because they were curious to see this strange tsar. And he, too, was curious to hear about this great Queen Elizabeth. So he sent ambassadors to visit her. Elizabeth gave them a magnificent entertainment with huge feasts and bear-baiting shows, and sent them back with presents for the tsar. He was so pleased that he promised to help all English traders and sailors who adventured to Russia and gave them freedom to go wherever they liked.

A Scottish ambassador at court

One of the foreign visitors Elizabeth liked best was Sir James Melville, sent as an ambassador from her cousin, Mary Queen of Scots (whose mother had been sister of Henry VIII). You may be surprised to hear a Scotsman called a foreigner, but England and Scotland were then two separate countries, ruled by these two queens. They pretended to be most loving, but each really feared the other. Elizabeth feared that Mary would try to make herself queen of England; Mary feared that Elizabeth would stir up the Scottish people against her. However, they sent each other loving messages and beautiful presents. Melville was a good messenger to send to Elizabeth because he knew how to make graceful speeches. He had travelled abroad, so the Queen was able to show off by talking to him in French, German and Italian.

She put on a different dress each day during his first visit and was delighted when he said that the Italian style suited her best because it showed off her curling red-gold hair. He described their conversation:

> 'She asked me whether my queen's hair or hers was best and which of them was fairest. I said she was the fairest queen in England and mine in Scotland. Yet she persisted. I answered, they were both the fairest

ladies in their countries; that Her majesty was whiter but my queen was very lovely. She inquired which of them was of higher stature [taller]? I said, my queen. Then said Elizabeth, she is too high, for I myself am neither too high nor too low.'

Later Melville was taken to stand outside the Queen's door to hear her playing on the **virginals** without being seen. He says:

'After I had heard awhile, seeing her back was toward the door, I ventured within and stood hearing her play excellently well; but she left off immediately so soon as she saw me. She asked how I came there? I said that as I passed the door I heard such music as delighted me, whereby I was drawn in ere [before] I knew how. Then she sat down low upon a cushion. She inquired if my queen or she played best? In that I found myself obliged to give her the praise. Then she inquired of me whether she or my queen danced best? I answered that my queen danced not so high or **disposedly** as she did.'

You can find out what happened to Mary Queen of Scots later on in another *Then and There* book.

Things to do

1. Find out why Russia was called Muscovy in the sixteenth century.
2. Why do you think Elizabeth wanted to leave the question of her marriage undecided?
3. Why were Elizabeth's questions to Sir James Melville (pages 48–49) awkward ones for him to answer? Was he a flatterer? Do you think Elizabeth was a vain woman?

8 Court festivities

Elizabeth loved plays and **masques** (in which dancers were masked or disguised). Her Master of the Revels chose plays and masques to be acted at Court and arranged the costumes. His accounts show us the kind of things he had to buy. Once he paid £1 10s for a machine to make lightning and thunder.

Christmas masques

For weeks before Christmas the Master of the Revels and his servants were busy making costumes and exciting things like cardboard dragons, fairy coaches and castles on wheels. The courtiers loved dressing-up and came to the Master asking for the strangest clothes. They practised in private, for the masque had to be kept a secret until the performance. Imagine lords dressed as **Moors** bursting into the midst of the Court. Their faces and arms were covered with black velvet, their hair was made of black muslin and they were dressed in blue velvet, with red and silver decorations. They had torch-bearers with head-dresses of crimson satin and they danced madly by the flickering light of torches until all the Court joined in.

Another time the dancers and Foresters were in green satin with crimson cloaks, while Wild Men of the Woods, hung with moss and ivy, carried the torches. One New Year's Day there was a masque with a mock snow-storm of sweets.

Acting plays before the Queen

There were companies of actors who travelled about performing plays in big houses or inn courtyards or in the

Here people feast while musicians play and revellers dance in a circle.

new London theatres. The Master of the Revels would send to the companies with good actors commanding them to rehearse their plays to him so that he could choose those he thought the Queen would like best. The players, of course, were eager to come, for if Elizabeth liked their plays other people would want to see them too. The Master would rehearse the chosen plays very carefully for he knew that the Queen might stop the play in the middle if it did not please her. Can you picture her in the Great Hall of her palace, seated on a throne in front of the stage? The

51

courtiers would gather round and then the play would begin.

The actors usually found a nobleman to be their patron. One company belonged to Robert Dudley, Earl of Leicester. The most famous one had the Queen herself for patron. They wore red coats and were called Queen Elizabeth's Men. William Shakespeare belonged to a company called the Lord Chamberlain's Men. Shakespeare wrote *The Midsummer Night's Dream* specially for a grand wedding which Elizabeth attended.

The Children of the Chapel

In Elizabeth's Court there were twelve choirboys called the Children of the Chapel. The youngest was about ten and the eldest about thirteen. They sang in all the chapel services. They lived with a schoolmaster who taught them arithmetic, spelling, dancing, singing and music. He also taught them to act plays. Sometimes they had a hard life, getting wet and cold as they travelled about with the Court, sometimes not getting enough to eat. But they had a splendid uniform – orange-tawny suits embroidered in silver, golden hose and scarlet cloaks – and when they appeared before the brilliant Queen and Court, I think they might have forgotten the hardships in the thrill of acting their plays.

Making music

At all times the Queen and her Court loved listening to music and making it themselves. Nearly everyone had been taught to sing and many people learnt to play a musical instrument. If you could not sight-read a part-song people thought you had been badly educated. Many songs had four parts and the music was printed so that the different parts could be read by four people sitting round a square table. One book of twenty-five songs, written by some of the best English composers, was called *The*

Elizabethan musicians. The lady in the middle is playing the virginals, like Queen Elizabeth. What instrument do you think the man on the right has?

Triumphs of Oriana. The name Oriana stood for Elizabeth and all the songs were in her honour.

Many of the ladies imitated Elizabeth in playing the virginals, an instrument which was like a very small piano. People also played lutes, sackbuts, trumpets, pipes and drums.

One of Elizabeth's musicians was William Byrd. He became the Master of the Chapel Royal and wrote glorious anthems for the Queen's choir to sing. Byrd wanted everyone to be able to sing well. So at the beginning of a book of his songs he wrote down all the reasons he could think of to persuade people how good it was to sing properly. Here are some of his reasons.

1. It is a knowledge easily taught and quickly learnt.
2. The exercise of singing is delightful and good to preserve the health of Man.

3. It doth strengthen the chest and open up the pipes.
4. It is a singular good remedy for stammering.
5. It is the best means to get a perfect pronunciation.
6. It is the only way to find out where Nature hath bestowed a good voice.
7. There is no music of instruments which is as good as that made by the voice of men.
8. The better the voice is, the better it is to honour and serve God with.

   Since singing is so good a thing
   I wish all men would learn to sing.

Things to do

1. Find out which play by Shakespeare has in it Nick Bottom and his friends who act before a king and queen. What play do they act?

2. Write a short story about the Children of the Chapel.

3. Put Byrd's eight reasons into your own words. If you like singing, write down your own reasons for doing it.

4. Why do you think England was called 'a nest of singing birds' in Elizabeth's time?

9 Elizabeth and her Parliaments

When the Queen opened Parliament she rode to Westminster in a coach, dressed in her crimson velvet Parliament robe; she wore the royal crown and carried the sceptre and orb, while in front of her the sword of state was carried. She opened Parliament with a speech which she composed herself and then the Lords and Commons began their discussions.

At Elizabeth's first Parliament in 1559 they had to decide what kind of services to have in the churches. With Elizabeth's consent, the Lords and Commons agreed to use the Book of Common Prayer which is almost the same as the one sometimes used in the Church of England today.

The Commons petition the Queen

Then the Speaker of the Commons sent a message to the Queen asking if the Commons could present an important petition to her. She received them in the great gallery at Whitehall and there the Speaker solemnly begged Elizabeth to marry. The Queen thought a little while and then she made a speech saying that whether she married or not she would always try to serve England well. Here is part of her speech.

> 'And [if I marry] whoever I shall choose I trust he shall be such as shall be as careful of the realm and you as I myself. And if it shall please Almighty God to continue me still to live out of marriage, yet in the end this shall be to me sufficient that a marble stone shall say that a Queen lived and died a Virgin. And here I end and take your coming unto me in good part and give you all my hearty thanks.'

Elizabeth opening Parliament in 1584 in the 'Painted Chamber'. Find the royal coat of arms and the woolsack. Where are the Commons? This picture comes from a description of Parliament written at the time.

Elizabeth liked to make a speech with lots of fine words in which she did not really promise anything. So here she is very cleverly saying neither 'Yes nor No' to Parliament about marrying.

56

The Commons went on asking Elizabeth either to marry or to decide who was to succeed her as king or queen. Sometimes she answered them pleasantly, sometimes she was angry with them because she thought they were interfering in her business. In most things she got her own way.

Elizabeth could get very angry indeed with people who did not see things her way. She could snap them off in mid-speech, order them to their knees to beg her pardon, threaten them with prison. She was good at flattering the politicians when they had the power, too. Above all, she kept people guessing about the way she would behave:

> 'When she smiled, it was pure sunshine that everyone did choose to **bask** in if they could; but by and bye came a storm from a sudden gathering of clouds and the thunder fell in wondrous manner on all alike.'

The Commons thanks the Queen

In 1601, near the end of Elizabeth's life, the Commons gave her some money from taxes and made a speech saying how grateful they were for all her care of England:

> 'Because no age hath ever produced so much happiness under any Prince's reign nor so much continual gracious care for our preservation as your Majesty hath showed in this time of your most happy government, therefore do we with all duty and humble affection . . . present to your sacred Majesty four entire subsidies [taxes] . . . towards your Highness' great expenses for our defence.'

Things to do

1. Why was Parliament so anxious for Elizabeth to marry?
2. Put Elizabeth's reply to Parliament (page 55) into your own words.

10 Epilogue

Elizabeth grows old

All things must have an end, even the reign of a great queen. Elizabeth had come to the throne in 1558 at the age of twenty-five. By 1603 she was an old woman. She had saved England from being conquered by France or Spain. She had seen great and exciting days. Now many of the people she had trusted were dead: Lord Burghley, the Earl of Leicester and many more. There were younger men all round her.

For a long time she pretended that she was not growing old and that she never got ill. When her hair began to go grey she took to wearing red wigs and she stopped looking in the mirror. When people said she was too old to go on a progress, she travelled round the country in the old style. Those that were too aged or ill, she said, could stay at home, but she would go.

Elizabeth finally gives in

At last she could pretend no longer: it was obvious that she was going to die. She would not go to bed but lay on cushions in her Privy Chamber. One of her young courtiers, Sir Robert Carey, tells us how he visited her there:

> 'When I came to Court I found the Queen **ill-disposed** and she kept to her inner lodging; yet she, hearing of my arrival, sent for me. I found her sitting low upon her cushions. She called me to her. I kissed her hand and told her it was my chiefest happiness to see her in safety and in health, which I wished might long continue. She took me by the hand and wrung it hard

and said: "No, Robin, I am not well," and then talked with me of her illness and how her heart had been sad and heavy for ten or twelve days, and in her **discourse** she fetched forty or fifty great sighs.'

Elizabeth's death

When she grew worse, her Councillors asked her who was to be king after her. They thought she nodded when the name of King James of Scotland was spoken. Finally, the Archbishop of Canterbury kneeled beside her. He told her plainly that though she had been long a great queen here upon earth, yet shortly she was to give an account of her **stewardship** to the King of Kings.

This is how a Londoner recorded Elizabeth's death: 'This morning about three o'clock her Majesty departed this life, mildly like a lamb, easily like a ripe apple from the tree.' So Queen Elizabeth died. Immediately the news came, Sir Robert Carey jumped on his horse and rode away to Scotland to tell King James. He galloped night and day, for he wanted to be the first to tell the King. James had been waiting eagerly for this moment and as soon as possible he set out to ride into his new kingdom.

Elizabeth's funeral

For the moment, however, people in England thought chiefly of how they had lost their Queen. There was a solemn and splendid funeral procession from Whitehall to Westminster Abbey. First came crowds of poor men and women and palace servants, then the heralds carrying the Dragon and Lion standards, and then the Children of the Chapel in white surplices, singing. After these came the Lord Mayor and Aldermen of London and all the nobles and bishops. Then came the coffin, covered with purple velvet, on a **chariot** drawn by four horses covered with black velvet. On the coffin lay a figure of the Queen, dressed in her Parliament robes, with her crown and

Part of Elizabeth's funeral procession.

sceptre. Over it was a canopy carried by six knights and six earls. After the coffin came the Queen's Master of Horse, leading her own special horse, her Gentlemen and all her Ladies and Maids of Honour. The streets were lined with people and there was a great sigh as the procession passed.

So Queen Elizabeth I was buried with great ceremony and honour. Then everyone turned to see what kind of a king this James VI of Scotland, now James I of England as well, was going to be.

Things to do

1. Find out who King James' mother was (see page 48). Why had he a right to become king of England?

2. Why was Sir Robert Carey in such a hurry to get to Scotland? Look again at what he said to Elizabeth (pages 58–59). Was he being honest with her?

3. What did the Archbishop of Canterbury mean when he spoke to Elizabeth (page 59)?

4. When an important person dies today there is an account of him or her (called an obituary) in the newspapers. Write an obituary for Queen Elizabeth I.

How do we know?

Sources are writings and things which belong to the times we want to find out about. Here is a list of the sources which told me about Queen Elizabeth and her Court:
1. Portraits of Elizabeth and famous people in her reign. Many of these are in the National Portrait Galley in London which you can visit.
2. Elizabeth's own letters, speeches and accounts.
3. Letters and diaries of her statesmen and other people of the time.
4. Descriptions of her Court, especially those written by foreign visitors like Hentzner and Melville.
5. Descriptions of her progresses written by people of the time.
6. Drawings of great processions by people who saw them.
7. Plays and poems by famous writers like Shakespeare, Spenser, Sidney.
8. Music by famous musicians of the time and old musical instruments.
9. Royal palaces still standing and old drawings of those pulled down.
10. Elizabethan furniture still kept in houses or museums.

Glossary

ambassador	messenger to the Queen from a foreign country
to **banquet**	to feast
to **bask**	to warm yourself
Roman Catholic	the part of the Christian religion of which the Pope is head
chamber	room
chandlery	place where candles are sold
chariot	special kind of carriage
comfit	a fruit or nut coated with sugar
corrupted	bribed – to betray the Queen
cupola	small dome
to **dedicate**	here means to write a book or poem in honour of a particular person
discourse	talk
disposedly	gracefully
to **doff**	to take off
to **don**	to put on
doublet	man's close fitting garment for the top half of his body
ermine	white fur
etiquette	rules of polite behaviour
farthingale	woman's petticoat stiffened with hoops
groom	servant
halberd	long-handled weapon with an axe head
Hercules	ancient Greek hero famous for his great strength
hose	breeches
ill-disposed	here means ill
inventory	list of possessions
joust	mock fight
kirtle	lady's dress in two parts, a bodice and a skirt open down the front
lance	spear
litter	here means a covered chair carried on two poles in which people travelled
lute	early musical instrument, like a guitar

mantle	cloak
masque	dance or play in which the players disguise themselves
Mercury	swift messenger of the gods in old Greek stories
Moors	dark-coloured men from North Africa
musket	an early kind of gun
Neptune	god of the sea in old Greek stories
orb	golden ball with cross on top carried by king or queen
pageant	splendid show
patron	rich or important man who helps someone who is poorer
peerless	more beautiful than any other
pelican	bird
petition	request, often put into writing
phoenix	mythical bird which burned and rose again from the flames
pike	weapon like a spear
privy	private
Protestant	part of the Christian religion which separated from the Catholic Church
revel	here means an entertainment
rustic	country peasant
sackbut	kind of trumpet, like a trombone
scabbard	case for a sword
sceptre	short stick of gold and jewels carried by a king or queen as a sign of power
to **skirmish**	practise military manoeuvres
squib	fire work
statesman	someone who gives wise advice about government
stature	height of a person
stewardship	here means the way the Queen had governed
suitor	here means someone who asks a lady to marry him
tawny	yellow-brown
tilt yard	yard specially arranged for mock fights
Titan	the sun
turret	small tower
usher	servant who guarded the door and brought visitors into the Queen's presence
virginals	very early kind of small piano

Index

actors, 50–2
Anne, Queen of England, 5
Armada, the, 36
Ascham, Roger, 5

beggars, 42–3
Byrd, William, 53–4

Carey, Sir Robert, 58–9
Catherine, Queen of England, 5
Cecil, Sir William (Lord
  Burghley), 58
Chancellor, Lord, 19
Children of the Chapel, 52, 59
clothes, 14, 16, 19, 26, 36–7
Court, 10, 19–24; dancing at,
  22–4; festivities at, 50–4
courtiers, 15, 19, 34–40, 50

dancing, 22–4, 51
Dudley, Sir Robert (Earl of
  Leicester), 37–8, 43, 52, 58
Edward VI, King of England,
  5–8
Elizabeth I, Queen of England,
  as princess, 5–9; learning of,
  5–6, 18, 20, 29–30; coronation
  of, 10–11; appearance of,
  11–14, 19; portraits of, 11–13;
  presents to, 15–16; amusements
  of, 16–17, 22–6, 50–3;
  servants of 21–2; signature of,
  22; ceremonies of, 26–8;
  palaces of, 29–33; statesmen
  of, 34–40; progresses of,
  41–5; suitors of, 46–7; foreign
  ambassadors to, 47–9;
  parliaments of, 55–7; death
  and funeral of, 58–60

food, 21
foreign visitors, 18–20, 29–30,
  46–9

George, St., 27

Greenwich Palace, 25, 32
Grey, Lady Jane, 8

Hampton Court Palace, 30–2
Hatton, Sir Christopher (Lord
  Chencellor), 36
Henry VIII, King of England, 5, 30
hunting, 9, 17
Hilliard, Nicholas, 37

James VI of Scotland and I of
  England, 59–60

London, people of, 8, 10, 24–5

Mary, Queen of England, 5,
  8–9, 34
Mary, Queen of Scots, 34, 48–9
masques, 50–2
Master of the Revels, 50–1
Maunday Thursday, 26–7
Melville, James, 48–9
music, 25, 49, 51–4

Nonsuch Palace, 32–3

Parliament, 55–7
Philip, King of Spain, 34

Raleigh, Sir Walter, 38–9
Richmond Palace, 30–2

Shakespeare, William, 52
Sidney, Sir Philip, 26, 39
Spenser, Edmund, 39–40

Thames, the, 9, 25
tournaments, 25–30
Tower of London, 8, 10

Walsingham, Sir Francis, 35
Westminster, 10, 59
Whitehall Palace, 29–30, 59
Windsor Castle, 32
Wolsey, Thomas, 30
Woodstock Palace, 8

Yeomen of the Guard, 20